CENTAUREA
FANCY MIXED

BURT'S SEED
FOR QUALITY

D1360774

IAS

Seeds of Kindness

Garden Thoughts for the Heart

A Special Gift
For:

_____

From:

_____

Date:

_____

Cherished Moments Gift Books

A Basket of Friends

Merry Christmas With Love

Once Upon a Memory
Reflections of Childhood

Seeds of Kindness
Garden Thoughts for the Heart

Sweet Rose of Friendship

Tea for Two
Taking Time for Friends

Where Angels Dwell
*A Treasury of Hope,
Inspiration and Blessing*

Seeds of Kindness

Garden Thoughts for the Heart

Featuring the Inspirational Writings of Celia Thaxter

Edited by Caroline Burns

Brownlow
Brownlow Publishing Company, Inc.

To Plant a Seed

The very act of planting a seed in the earth has in it to me something beautiful. I always do it with a joy that is largely mixed with awe. I watch my garden beds after they are sown, and think how one of God's exquisite miracles is going on beneath the dark earth out of sight. I never forget my planted seeds. Often I wake in the night and think how the rains and the dews have reached to the dry shell and softened it; how the spirit of life begins to stir within, and the individuality of the plant to assert itself; how it is thrusting two hands forth from the imprisoning husk, one, the root, to grasp the earth, to hold itself firm and absorb its food, the other stretching above to find the light, that it may drink in the breeze and sunshine and so climb to its full perfection of beauty. It is curious that the leaf should so love the light and the root so hate it.

— CELIA THAXTER

Garden Hearts

Kind hearts are the gardens.

Kind thoughts are the roots.

Kind words are the flowers.

Take care of the gardens,

and keep them from weeds.

Fill, fill them with flowers,

kind words, and kind deeds.

HENRY WADSWORTH LONGFELLOW

Little Cottage Garden

I have learned much from the little cottage gardens that help to make our English waysides the prettiest in the temperate world. One can hardly go into the smallest cottage garden without learning or observing something new. It may be some two plants growing beautifully together by some happy chance, or a pretty mixed tangle of creepers, or something that one always thought must have a south wall doing better on an east one. But eye and brain must be alert to receive the impression and studious to store it, to add to the hoard of experience. And it is important to train oneself to have a good flower-eye; to be able to see at a glance what flowers are good and which are unworthy, and why, and to keep an open mind about it, not to be swayed by the petty tyrannies of the "florist" or show judge; for, though some part of his judgment may be sound, he is himself a slave to rules, and must go by points which are defined arbitrarily and rigidly.

       GERTRUDE JEKYLL

The Tradition of Excellence

Gardening is a luxury occupation: an ornament, not a necessity, of life. The farmer is not at all concerned with the eventual beauty of his corn as a feature in the landscape, though, indeed, he gets a certain satisfaction out of it, as he leans against his gate on a summer evening, and sees his acres gently curving to the breeze. Still, beauty is not his primary aim; the gardener's is. Fortunate gardener, who may preoccupy himself solely with beauty in these difficult and ugly days! He is one of the few people left in this distressful world to carry on the tradition of elegance and charm. A useless member of society, considered in terms of economics, he must not be denied his rightful place. He deserves to share it, however humbly, with the painter and the poet.

— VITA SACKVILLE-WEST

Culture of the Earth

I have often thought that if heaven had given me a choice of my position and calling, it should have been on a rich spot of earth, well watered, and near a good market for the productions of the garden. No occupation is so delightful to me as the culture of the earth, and no culture comparable to that of the garden. Such a variety of subjects, some one always coming to perfection, the failure of one thing repaired by the success of another, and instead of one harvest a continued one through the year. Under a total want of demand except for our family table, I am still devoted to the garden. But though an old man, I am but a young gardener.

THOMAS JEFFERSON

*The first gathering
of the garden in May
of salads, radishes and herbs
made me feel like a
mother about her baby —
how could anything
so beautiful be mine.
And this emotion
of wonder filled me
for each vegetable as it
was gathered every year.
There is nothing that
is comparable to it,
as satisfactory or as thrilling,
as gathering the vegetables
one has grown.*

ALICE B. TOKLAS

The world has different owners at sunrise....
Even your own garden does not belong to you.
Rabbits and blackbirds have the lawns;
a tortoise-shell cat who never appears in daytime
patrols the brick walls, and a golden-tailed pheasant
glints his way through the iris spears.

 ❧ Anne Morrow Lindbergh

Yes! in the poor man's garden grow,
Far more than herbs and flowers,
Kind thoughts, contentment,
peace of mind,
And joy for weary hours.

 ❧ Mary Howitt

The late summer garden
has a tranquility found
no other time of year.

 ❧ William Longgood

*Whoever sows sparingly will also reap sparingly,
and whoever sows generously
will also reap generously.*

— 2 CORINTHIANS 9:6

The love of gardening is a seed that once sown never dies.

— GERTRUDE JEKYLL

Like life, few gardens have only flowers.

— ANONYMOUS

*Who loves a garden still his Eden keeps,
Perennial pleasures plants,
and wholesome harvest reaps.*

— AMOS BRONSON ALCOTT

*Kindness is like a rose,
which though easily crushed
and fragile, yet speaks a
language of silent power.*

— FRANCES J. ROBERTS

*Can you ever
remember a time
when you regretted
having said a kind word?*

The First Seeds

I don't know why but I somehow managed to let nasturtiums slip from consciousness, like old friends long neglected. And nasturtiums and I go very far back indeed. They were the first seeds my mother let me plant, when I was no more than five years old. Her choice was excellent. The seeds are large, about the size of an English pea, but corky and wrinkled. Children know for certain that they are planting something, with none of the doubt that might accompany the planting of petunias or nicotiana seeds, which look like fine brown dust.

ALLEN LACY

The Caretaker

You care for the land and water it;
you enrich it abundantly.
The streams of God are filled with water
to provide the people with grain,
for so you have ordained it.
You drench its furrows and level its ridges;
you soften it with showers and bless its crops.

You crown the year with your bounty,
and your carts overflow with abundance.
The grasslands of the desert overflow;
the hills are clothed with gladness.
The meadows are covered with flocks
and the valleys are mantled with grain;
they shout for joy and sing.

PSALM 65:9-13

The Sowing of Seeds

Yes, the sowing of a seed seems a very simple matter, but I always feel as if it were a sacred thing among the mysteries of God. Standing by that space of blank and motionless ground, I think of all it holds for me of beauty and delight, and I am filled with joy at the thought that I may be the one to whom power is given to summon so sweet a pageant from the silent and passive soil.

I bring a mat from the house and kneel by the smooth bed of mellow brown earth, lay a narrow strip of board across it a few inches from one end, draw a furrow firmly and evenly in the ground along the edge of the board, repeating this until the whole bed is grooved at equal distances across its entire length. Into these straight furrows the living seeds are dropped, the earth replaced over them (with a depth of about twice their diameter), and the board laid flat with gentle pressure over all the surface till it is perfectly smooth again. Then must the whole be lightly and carefully watered. With almost all the seeds sown in this bird-blest and persecuted little garden, I am obliged to lay newspapers or some protection over the planted beds, and over these again sheets of wire netting, to keep off the singing sparrows till the seeds are safely sprouted.

Last year, one morning early in May, I put a border of Mignonette seeds round every flower bed. When I came to the garden again in the afternoon, it was alive with flirting wings and tails and saucy beaks and bright eyes, and stout little legs and claws scratching like mad; all white-throats and song-sparrows, and hardly a seed had these merry little marauders left in the ground.

CELIA THAXTER

A Little Kindness

Kind words toward those
you daily meet,

Kind words and
actions right,

Will make this life of ours
most sweet,

Turn darkness into light.

ᴵꜱᴀᴀᴄ Wᴀᴛᴛꜱ

Lord of the Garden

We are the roadside flowers
Straying from garden grounds;
Lovers of idle hours,
Breakers of ordered bounds.
If only the earth will feed us,
If only the wind be kind,
We blossom for those who need us,
The stragglers left behind.
And lo, the Lord of the Garden,
He makes His sun to rise,
And His rain to fall like pardon
On our dusty paradise.
On us He has laid the duty —
The task of the wandering breed —
To better the world with beauty,
Wherever the way may lead.
Who shall inquire of the season,
Or question the wind where it blows?
We blossom and ask no reason,
The Lord of the Garden knows.

BLISS CARMEN

*If you wish to make anything grow, you must
understand it in a very real sense. "Green fingers" are a fact,
and a mystery only to the unpracticed. But green fingers
are the extensions of a verdant heart.*

☙ RUSSELL PAGE

*Life is short and we have not too much time for gladdening
the hearts of those who are traveling the dark way with us.
Oh, be swift to love! Make haste to be kind!*

☙ HENRI FRÉDÉRIC AMIEL

*In my garden there is a large place for sentiment.
My garden of flowers is also my garden of thoughts
and dreams. The thoughts grow as freely as the flowers,
and the dreams are as beautiful.*

☙ ABRAM LINWOOD URBAN

Oh, Adam was a gardener, and God who made him sees
That half a proper gardener's work is done upon his knees,
So when your work is finished,
you can wash your hands and pray
For the Glory of the Garden, that it may not pass away!

— RUDYARD KIPLING

I wish everybody had a garden,
And would work in it himself.
The world would grow sweeter-tempered at once.

— ANNA WARNER

So deeply is the gardener's instinct implanted in my soul,
I really love the tools with which I work — the iron fork,
the spade, the hoe, the rake, the trowel, and
the watering-pot are pleasant objects in my eyes.

— CELIA THAXTER

To Be in England

Oh, to be in England
Now that April's there,
And whoever wakes in England
Sees, some morning, unaware,
That the lowest boughs
and the brushwood sheaf
Round the elm-tree bole are in tiny leaf,
While the chaffinch sings
on the orchard bough
In England — now!

ROBERT BROWNING

To cultivate
a Garden
is to
walk
with
God.

CHRISTIAN BOVEE

Gardening
by oneself
is so lovely,
and so easy
a thing,
that I
would fain
have
everybody
try it.

ANNA WARNER

Those who sow
seeds of kindness
will have a
perpetual harvest.

True to the Seed

Any one seed may be too old to sprout
or inferior in some way, but it will never
try to be something it isn't fitted to be.
A man may study to be a surgeon when
he should have been a shoemaker,
a talented painter may spend his life
trying to convince himself and his fellows
that he is a lawyer, but a turnip seed
will never attempt to grow into an ear of corn.
If you plant a good turnip seed properly a
turnip is what you will get every single time.

RUTH STOUT

When I am **alone** the flowers are really seen;
I can pay **attention** to them
                    They are felt as **presences**.
    Without them I would die.
            Why do I say that?
        Partly because they **change** before my eyes.
They **live** and **die**
        in a few days;
    they keep me
        closely in **touch**
with **process**,
        with **growth**,
    and also with **dying**.
I am **floated** on their moments.

    MAY SARTON

Silence Before Sunrise

As I work among my flowers, I find myself talking to them, reasoning and remonstrating with them, and adoring them as if they were human beings. Much laughter I provoke among my friends by so doing, but that is of no consequence. We are on such good terms, my flowers and I!

In the sweet silence before sunrise, standing in the garden I watch the large round shield of the full moon slowly fading in the west from copper to brass and then to whitest silver, throwing across a sea of glass its long, still reflection, while the deep, pure sky takes on a rosy warmth of color from the approaching sun. Soon an insufferable glory burns on the edge of the eastern horizon; up rolls the great round red orb and sets the dew twinkling and sparkling in a thousand rainbows, sending its first rejoicing rays over the wide face of the world.

When in these fresh mornings I go into my garden before any one is awake, I go for the time being into perfect happiness. In this hour divinely fresh and still, the fair face of every flower *salutes me with a silent joy that fills me with infinite content; each gives me its color, its grace, its perfume, and enriches me with the consummation of its beauty. All the cares, perplexities, and griefs of existence, all the burdens of life slip from my shoulders and leave me with the heart of a little child that asks nothing beyond its present moment of innocent bliss.*

These myriad beaming faces turned to mine seem to look at me with blessing eyes. I feel the personality of each flower, and I find myself greeting them as if they were human. "Good-morning, beloved friends! Are all things well with you? And are you tranquil and bright? and are you happy and beautiful?" They stand in their peace and purity and lift themselves to my adoring gaze as if they knew my worship, —so calm, so sweet, so delicately radiant, I lose myself in the tranquillity of their happiness. They seem like sentient beings, as if they knew me and loved me, not indeed as I love them, but with almost a reliance on my sympathy and care, and a pleasure in my delight in them.

ᔌ CELIA THAXTER

A Garden Stroll

For it seems that proper gardeners never sit in their gardens.
Dedicated and single-minded, the garden draws them into its
embrace where their passions are never assuaged unless they
are on their knees. But for us, the unserious, the improper
people, who plant and drift, who prune and amble, we fritter
away little dollops of time in sitting about our gardens.
Benches for sunrise, seats for contemplation, resting perches
for the pure sublimity of smelling the evening air or merely
ruminating about a distant shrub. We are the unorthodox
gardeners who don't feel compulsion to pull out campion
among the delphiniums; we can idle away vacantly small
chunks of time without fretting about an outcrop of butter-
cups groping at the pulsatillas. Freedom to loll goes with
random gardening, it goes with the modicum of chaos which
I long to see here and there in more gardens.

MIRABEL OSLER

Kindness adds sweetness to everything.
It is kindness which makes life's capabilities blossom,
and paints them with their cheering hues,
and endows them with their invigorating presence.

FREDERICK W. FABER

You may go into the field or down the lane,
but don't go into Mr. McGregor's garden.

BEATRIX POTTER

Into My Garden

My heart shall be thy garden.
Come, my own,
Into thy garden;
thine be happy hours
Among my fairest thoughts,
my tallest flowers,
From root to crowning petal
thine alone.

ALICE MEYNELL

Without love and kindness, life is cold, selfish,
and uninteresting, and leads to distaste for everything.
With kindness, the difficult becomes easy, the obscure clear;
life assumes a charm and its miseries are softened.
If we knew the power of kindness,
we should transform this world into a paradise.
CHARLES WAGNER

Always be a little kinder than necessary.
JAMES M. BARRIE

The man who has planted
a garden feels that he has
done something for the
good of the whole world.
CHARLES DUDLEY WARNER

There's nothing so kingly
as kindness,
And nothing so loyal
as truth.
ALICE CARY

Childhood Memories

When I was a little girl,
my mother took great pains
to interest me in learning to
know the birds and wild flowers
and in planting a garden.
I thought that roots and
bulbs and seeds were as
wonderful as flowers, and the
Latin names on seed packages
as full of enchantment as the
counting-out rhymes that children
chant in the spring. I remember
the first time I planted seeds.
My mother asked me if
I knew the Parable of the Sower.
I said I did not, and she took me
into the house and read it to me.

ELIZABETH LAWRENCE

Grandmother's Garden

O gardener, let the scarlet poppies grow!
Keep the marigolds, the hollyhocks and phlox;
Leave the beds of purple pansies blooming low,
With the sweet little pinks and four-o'clocks.

Spare a place for the southernwood and balm,
For the mint, and the tansy, and the sage;
We would not have these treasures come to harm
That cheered and soothed her feeble, failing age.

Through these trim little aisles she used to walk,
In the fresh early mornings of the spring,
And welcome every shoot and budding stalk,
And taught these morning-glories how to cling.

Here are roses dewy, fragrant, white and red;
Here are lilies dainty-chaliced, fair and tall.
Were there ever sweeter, richer perfumes shed?
Were there ever fairer blossoms made to fall?

The world is wide, and in the farthest lands
Are lovely things that blossom in the dew;
But these — why, they grew beneath her hands!
We still will keep them sacred — would not you?

ANNA BOYNTON AVERILL

Every time I go into a garden where the man or woman who owns it has a passionate love of the earth and of growing things, I find that I have come home. In whatsoever land or clime or race, in whatsoever language, we speak a common tongue; the everlasting processes of earth bind us as one, stronger than Leagues or Covenants can ever bind.

꙰ MARION CRAN

Most gardeners I know would recoil from the suggestion that gardening is therapy, but they must know in their hearts that it helps that part of the brain or soul that this materialistic, competitive, noisy culture tends to unravel or destroy altogether. It is an antidote for the way many must earn their living. A garden must be the final refuge from progress and its relentless toll on "civilized" man.

꙰ WILLIAM LONGGOOD

Of Making Gardens

In England they have no sunlight or heat of a natural sunny sort, as indeed their gardeners are forever complaining. They make do — their gardens are the loveliest in the world today, largely because of the almost insurmountable challenge of the gray climate. There is nothing like impossibility for getting a gardener's energies up. Knowing that by nature they cannot (and do not) have anything, they have set themselves with zeal to the task of making gardens in the very face of the devil and the North Sea.

— HENRY MITCHELL

It is curious,
pathetic almost,
how deeply seated
in the human heart
is the liking
for gardens
and gardening.

ALEXANDER SMITH

The Path of Life

Thus, God's bright **sunshine** overhead,

God's **flowers** beside your feet,

The **path of life** that you must tread

Can little hold of **fear** or **dread**;

And by such pleasant
pathways led,

May all your
life be sweet.

❧ HELEN WAITHMAN

*There are few of us who cannot remember a front yard garden
which seemed to us a very paradise in childhood.*

❧ SARAH ORNE JEWETT

*The land produced vegetation:
plants bearing seed according to their kinds and
trees bearing fruit with seed in it according to their kinds.
And God saw that it was good.*

❧ GENESIS 1:12

*Everything that slows us down and forces patience,
everything that sets us back into the slow cycles of nature,
is a help. Gardening is an instrument of grace.*

❧ MAY SARTON

*Life is made up, not of great sacrifices or duties,
but of little things, in which smiles and kindness
and small obligations win and preserve the heart.*

❧ HUMPHREY DAVY

The Secret Is Love

He who is born with a silver spoon in his mouth is generally considered a fortunate person, but his good fortune is small compared to that of the happy mortal who enters this world with a passion for flowers in his soul. I use the word advisedly, though it seems a weighty one for the subject, for I do not mean a light or shallow affection, or even an æsthetic admiration; no butterfly interest, but a real love which is worthy of the name, which is capable of the dignity of sacrifice, great enough to bear discomfort of body and disappointment of spirit, strong enough to fight a thousand enemies for the thing beloved, with power, with judgment, with endless patience, and to give with everything else a subtler stimulus which is more delicate and perhaps more necessary than all the rest.

Often I hear people say, "How do you make your plants flourish like this?" as they admire the little flower patch I cultivate in summer, or the window gardens that bloom for me in the winter; "I can never make my plants blossom like this! What is your secret?" And I answer with one word, "Love." For that includes all, — the patience that endures continual trial, the constancy that makes perseverance possible, the power of foregoing ease of mind and body to minister to the necessities of the thing beloved, and the subtle bond of sympathy which is as important, if not more so, than all the rest.

❧ CELIA THAXTER

Working in the garden gives me a profound feeling of inner peace. Nothing here is in a hurry. There is no rush toward accomplishment, no blowing of trumpets. Here is the great mystery of life and growth. Everything is changing, growing, aiming at something, but silently, unboastfully, taking its time.

— RUTH STOUT

When I walk out of my house into my garden I walk out of my habitual self, my every-day thoughts, my customariness of joy and sorrow by which I recognise and assure myself of my own identity. These I leave behind me for a time, as the bather leaves his garments on the beach.

— ALEXANDER SMITH

Happy Hours Yet to Be

And so the ripe year wanes. From turfy slopes afar the breeze brings delicious, pungent, spicy odors from the wild Everlasting flowers, and the mushrooms are pearly in the grass. I gather the seed-pods in the garden beds, sharing their bounty with the birds I love so well, for there are enough and to spare for us all. Soon will set in the fitful weather, with

fierce gales and sullen skies and frosty air, and it will be time to tuck up safely my Roses and Lilies and the rest for their long winter sleep beneath the snow, where I never forget them, but ever dream of their wakening in happy summers yet to be.

᠆ CELIA THAXTER